T0145030

Dedicated to family and friends
for spurring me on to write this book.

1

The first summer in my mobilehome I built five rectangular flower boxes and planted two bougainvillea flowering shrubs in each one. All lined up and evenly spaced each one was open to the ground for the roots to grow.

Just outside my very long carport, they continued down the full length with white trellises attached inside every box. My plan was to entirely cover the carport with beauty and privacy. Now the newly planted bushes just needed some time to grow.

Early the following spring, a pair of birds flew into my neighborhood. I had never seen birds like these. So pretty. Wonder what kind they are? I noticed the two but didn't really watch them all that much. They took an immediate liking to my crepe myrtle. A mature tree located in the side yard next to the bougainvillea.

Both were coming and going, very busy working really hard at something.

I didn't stop to investigate what they were up to.

Then I saw it.

A nest...they had been in construction mode. Just as nature would have it, Mrs. laid her eggs.

Eggs...who would guess a bird would lay a soft-shelled egg with a baby in it.

Birds are SO Amazing

Shortly after, the two started fussing at me...but only when I got too close to

their tree!!!

Glad we don't lay eggs for our babies.

3

I had no reason to be in their territory and stayed in mine. Life was good. We were both content to live our respective lives. We co-inhabited successfully through the first set of babies hatching and flying away.

Lady bird laid another clutch. Diligently, the couple always let me know if I got too close. The male would fly around in front of me making a lot of distracting movements and noise to draw me away from the nest. The female stayed at her post on the eggs. After a period of time went by, they both flew off. I didn't see them anymore that year. Curious now, I decided to do a little research.

It was mockingbirds who had come to raise their family in my tree.

How sweet.

Springtime is when the bougainvillea wake up and grow rapidly. After another full year had lapsed the plants climbed to the top of the 7-foot white trellises. Filling out nicely, they progressively produced more and more bright beautiful fuchsia colored flowers.

Simultaneously a male mockingbird flew in and landed. I spotted him sitting on the chain link fence directly behind my mobilehome. He was a stately and nice looking bird. We made direct eye contact.

I looked at him...he looked at me.

And so... our relationship began.

He took quite a liking to my nice dense
bougainvillea bushes.
They were full of long dangerous thorns and
beautiful flowers.

Quite the perfect place he thought.

The male left and returned with a female, his wife
I presume. She looked exactly like him but smaller,
gentler, and much quieter.

Now there were two birds sitting on the fence.

Unbeknownst to be me...
        the two took up residence.

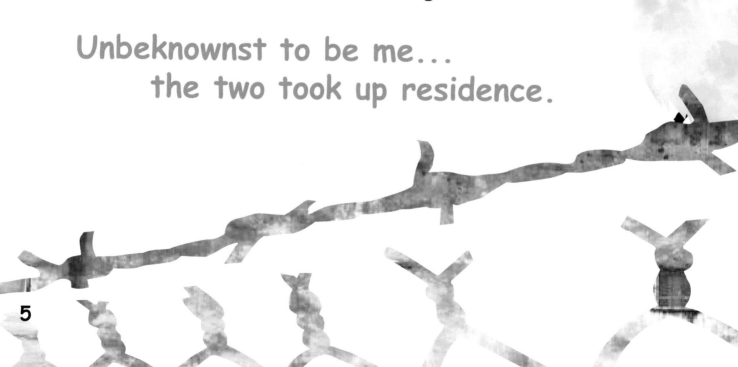

5

6

A nice little pair of finches moved into the top of my carport making it their spring home. Beautiful birds. Bright red feathers on the male and muted reds almost pink on the female.

Tiny little **beaks**, tiny little **peeps**, and **happy, happy.**

They were busy for several days gathering all their needed nesting materials. They flew in...they flew out.

Busy Busy Busy

The female laid her eggs and went about her egg duties. All that work, must be quite exhausting.

I loved watching them and hearing all their little sounds. I so enjoyed experiencing their daily activities.

7

Happy

Happy

Birds who
sing with
a sweet
melodious
sound

They sang when
they flew in.

They sang when...
they flew out.

About the same time a canary couple
flew in, new neighbors to the finches.
They choose a cozy apartment farther
down in the top of my carport. A
larger bird than the finch but still
on the small side.

Wonderful bright yellow feathers.

Eggs were laid.

The two went about their
parenting tasks. Little
tiny babies calling
" peep, peep, peep,

I'm hungry mom."

It was a busy
atmosphere with
mom and dad
frequently
coming and
going.

8

As I studied their ways, I started noticing different things. The pint-size finch with its little wings made a short chopping motion in the air. The canary had a more fluid and extended flap of the wings.

How fun

We all lived
together quite
nicely I thought.
I treasured working in
my yard and making it beautiful,
consequently I saw them frequently.
I didn't bother them...they didn't bother me.

Colorful happy joyful birds make me HAPPY!

It was the best of homelife and
nature living side by side.

Life was good.

9

One bright warm morning seeing their babies up in the carport corner reminded me of last summer. I shuddered at the memory. Spraying down my driveway, I saw what I thought was a hanging leaf in the top corner of my carport awning. Let me get that down. The water from the hose nozzle sprayed perfectly into the area. Huh, the leaf wasn't coming down? I sprayed it again. . .full force. Something wasn't right...I froze!!!

Upon further examination it was bobbing up and down. What I thought was a leaf was actually a baby...bird. Pausing now to see if it was still alive, I felt horrible. Looking carefully again. "Oh good," I sighed, it was still moving. There were in fact three fully drenched babies. They looked at me with stunned little eyes. I had almost drowned an entire nest of finches. Mom and dad weren't home but their babies got a shower.

Sorry...I won't do that again! Whew!!!

My back door opened out onto a porch with two sets of stairs. To the right, a small wooden gate opens into my carport where my truck is parked in the driveway.

On the opposite side, the steps lead down into the back yard where the trash bins were kept. Farther back around the corner of the house was my walk-in shed. The main access and working area were all within 10-15 feet of the long line of the beautiful bougainvillea.

A snug arrangement but all mine. It was where I lived and important to me.

I found their masterpiece quite by mistake. Taking out my trash one sunny spring morning, looking down I spotted an unfamiliar site.

It was a **bird nest**…it had to be the mockingbird couple. Everything was quiet. No birds were visible, so…let me take a closer looksee. It was skillfully built with twigs, pieces of twine, leaves, and various other items about the size of a small bowl. Just about waist high, it was cleverly nestled in a safe spot made easily accessible for him and the Mrs. newly built, empty and all ready for babies.

I smiled thinking how much I enjoyed birds.

What fun it would be to see them grow and develop right in my own driveway. A special treat for sure. Three different feathered couples raising their families in my carport. . . and me. I had the pleasure of watching them grow.

Later that same afternoon opening my back door, I spotted the male mockingbird sitting on the fence. As soon as he saw me his eyes locked on--following me everywhere I went.

With birds around me all the time, there was no real concern. I stepped down the porch stairs to my truck. Once ground level, something hit my head and then my ear. Immediately after something fluttered across my back. Flinching, I ducked down. On guard now, but still trying to figure out what was happening.

I saw him as soon as I turned around.

He came streaking down with lightning speed targeting me again...
I could feel him on my ear.

Wow! Oh Man!!!

They didn't even have
any eggs yet--much less babies.

How could I be a threat?
Is he just trying to scare me off?

Oh NO...A second attack!!! Looking up after,
his spread out tail and fully extended wings were all I
could see as he flew silently away from me.

With my heart racing I made it to the truck and drove off quickly. Once back
home from errands, still sitting in the driveway, I checked the surroundings.

I didn't see any birds and gathered my things. Relaxing, but only after
making it safely into the house. A little concerned now.

What if this becomes the norm?
How will I come and go for daily life?

14

My affection for birds spurred me on with curiosity. A few more days went by. I wanted to see if anything was happening in the nest. Standing on the back porch at the risk of being spotted, I tried to see into the nest but couldn't see anything.

Do I dare go over there?

Had they laid any eggs?
What color were they?
What size were they?

My yard was really starting to bloom and grow. Plants needed watering and grooming. My trash and yard waste went out to the street every Tuesday morning. The first time I took them out...no problem. Rolling the bins right past the empty nest there were no encounters from Mr. mockingbird. I have to say. . . I did wonder if it was safe to go down my own driveway to the trash.

This time we were ok.

I was mindful of the mockingbird couple but

"Come on!"

It was my house, I planted the bougainvillea.
I lived here first.

Occasionally, I would have a conversation with the mister telling him just that. Before the nest or any eggs, while watering the back yard I took the opportunity to talk to **him**. Looking at him sitting on the fence quite close to me, I said,

"We have to share."

Perched on the fence, he looked over. After studying me for a few minutes with his small round black eyes, he flew off.

I felt like we communicated.

Bravely and intentionally I walked down the driveway toward the gate...right by the nest. I needed to throw something in the trash bin. To my delight, there were three eggs. Small, turquoise and spotted. They did it! So exciting. Mr. stared me down the whole time but allowed me passage.

Did he want me to see his eggs?
I definitely knew he was there and he knew I was there.

With nervous anticipation, I practically ran back to the porch. Made it, relaxed and smiled at the thought of babies coming. Never having seen baby birds in a nest before...this was special.

16

He decided to get closer

17

I was in and out my back door frequently. Watering the yard, emptying the trash, going to the shed, or going to the truck. In addition, there was always a project of some kind in motion. Currently, the plan was to rebuild the deck on my small back porch. All the extensive rain that winter had warped out the top. With no foreseeable problems, I was on my way to the lumber store for wood and screws. Nothing much happened for the next few days. Observing the nest, the Mrs. was sitting diligently on her eggs. I savored watching all their various routines. They both shared in the responsibility of caring for the eggs. But with the newly inhabited nest...

Mr. became much-much-much more aggressive.

Now, going to my truck or working in my plants, he would dive at my head. **Then for diversity,** he would dive my face, my ear, my back…my shoulder. He was soooooo incredibly fast…and quiet.

That was the problem, I never knew when he was coming. Out came the fly swatter, but he was way too fast for that. Just swatting air. What will get his attention? Don't want to hurt him.   Ah... the broom.

Not even close.

The infuriating thing is that he always got me somewhere. Not a happy camper. He just waited until I turned my back...fast becoming a problem. As time progressed, I somehow managed to start my porch project. The Mrs. sitting faithfully on the nest would call him as soon as I stepped out the back door. At her request he came flying in. Mr. watched me with a fury. His little penetrating beady eyes were stuck on me and only me. He watched my every move. Previously, he sat on the chain link fence behind my house for dad duty. Now he decided to get closer. Mr. took a new spot on my fence where he could... **see me much better!!!**   **18**

Tuesday rolled around, trash day. Oh, my goodness I couldn't even get to the bins in my own yard. **He was at me with a vengeance.**

Time after time he came at me, silently diving from the sky toward me with his wings and tail feathers out.
He hit my head, my hair, my shoulder, and then my face.

Heart pounding, with my arm over my head, I bent down and moved quickly. I retreated to the house to regroup, smashed a big floppy hat on my head and went back out with the broom. The hat threw him off long enough for me to roll the trash bins thru the fence gate and down the driveway to the street.
Better use the front door. What a mess!!!

I am a most determined woman. It was time to pull off warped boards on my small back entry deck. My boxer was intrigued. Both mockingbirds were on duty and diligently watching. A high school student from the church came to help me. Interesting enough, as long as someone else was around there were no issues. After a short time, the rotten boards were off safely. Even though there was no interaction with the birds, they were both intently watching. Later that afternoon, I was able to roll trash bins back into their place inside the gate with...**no attacks.**

The next day the support beams were screwed into place for the deck. Mr. mockingbird left me alone for the most part. Oddly, he was a curious bird who liked to watch me, just like my dog, they both wondered what was going on. It was a relative uneventful day with my birds.
Nice for sure

He was a curious bird

20

The following morning was completely different. For unknown reasons to me, Mr. decided he didn't want me around and was on a mission to get rid of me. As I worked, with every movement, he was trying to get me. My floppy hat helped... but not much, it was old hat by now. Oh, but If I ever turned my back, he was all over me. Here came the wings, the feet and I'm not sure what else on my back. Each time he flew away from me. . . positioning for another attack, beautiful feathers were visible in his fanned tail and wings.

No matter how pretty he was...
I was not liking this bird. Enough of this!!!

Finishing the screws on the current brace, work came to a stop. Sitting on the fence directly across from me, he just glared. This mockingbird was only 8 inches tall, not a large bird by any means. However, his fearless determination to get rid of me was relentless.

His little black laser-beam eyes
radiated with a mean intensity. Scary!!!

Safe inside my house, searching the internet again. I needed some more information. How can I keep this mockingbird off of me??? One person suggested putting a nozzle on the hose to shoot a stream of water at them. I'm going to do that. It was soon hooked up with the sprayer on it. Sounded reasonable...but as I learned, it was like trying to spray a jet airplane. Mockingbirds are so incredibly fast. It became quite the game.

He always won.

Very maddening to say the least. He just waited until I wasn't looking and dove at me again. He was a master at catching me off guard. This relatively small bird was frightening me. It is a strange thing to have a bird silently target your head and face. Even so my love of birds caused me to be much more tolerant than others, I'm sure. **22**

The only way to continue work in my own back
yard on my own deck was, by hanging the hose on the railing
for quick access. At least this bird knew I had some form of minor
defense. **Do you think he cared?** He wasn't the slightest bit concerned

Mr. just waited me out.

So fearless now, I thought at one point, he would actually come all the
way in my back door. He just kept hopping closer and closer never taking
his eyes off me. With my floppy hat on, my daily routine soon consisted of
grabbing the hose frequently. Spraying out across the top of the bougainvillea
and into the street, with neighbors wondering what in the world was going on.
I was so embarrassed and felt ridiculous at how I was acting.

"Don't spray me!" Several times people yelled as they walked by.

Coming out the back door, the hose was immediately in my hand for my defense.

He knew I was coming. . . I knew he was coming.

23

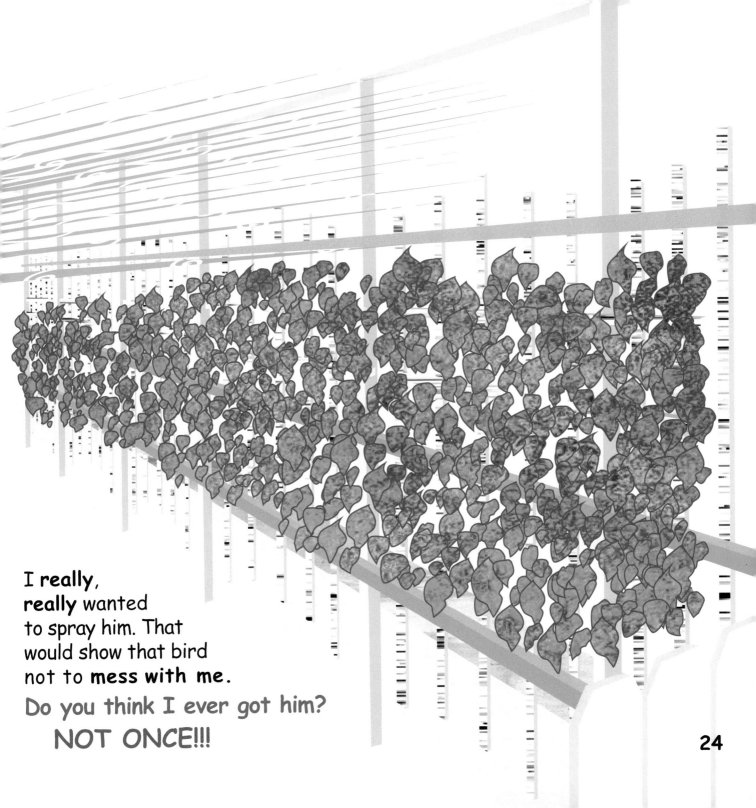

I **really,
really** wanted
to spray him. That
would show that bird
not to **mess with me.**

Do you think I ever got him?
NOT ONCE!!!

24

Somehow thru all the attacks, with shear tenacity, the supports were finished, and the top deck boards secured in place. Putting my tools away in the shed, I realized this was full-blown war.

How could I teach this bird a lesson?

Back to the Internet. Experts kept saying:

TRY not to get MAD at the mockingbird.

Too late!!!

I was MAD, plenty mad.

Expressing my anguish at work, a coworker suggested I call a bird sanctuary for help. The owner, Carla answering the phone asked me, "How tough are you?" "Quite tough," I responded. She proceeded to tell me her bird story. The property she owned had many acres where she rehabilitated birds of all kinds. A female hawk she nurtured back to health after her wing was damaged was later set free on the same property.

When this female hawk laid her eggs, she would not allow anyone close including Carla. Mom came down with open talons ready to hurt. She stayed away from the nest and waited for the babies to fly off from her own property. Now, she told me, you can

1. move the nest to another location   OR   2. destroy the babies.

My immediate thought was, "Both of those solutions will provoke more aggression from the mockingbirds **toward me!**"

Nope, can't do either one of those.

Well then Carla said - **give the couple adequate time**...about a month to raise their babies.

What...really
Tolerate this for a whole month?

Finally, Carla told me

Tear the Nest DOWN as soon as...the babies fly away!!!

Ok! NO problem just **one** set of babies, **right?**

26

I was tired of walking thru my own yard with a hose in my hands to ward off this insane mockingbird. In order to water anything, I always had to be on guard and never. . .never turn my back to him. Even so, he was so very clever and found other spots where he could get a running start at me before I could get the water going.

This bird was creative. I'll give him that. Mr. found other spots to perch -on top of my neighbor's antenna. He could see me, but I couldn't spray him. Well, I could have but at risk of spraying my neighbor while sitting on his porch with his dog. Seriously thought about it more than once, but finally decided against it.
This was my battle.
Really, really not liking this bird right now.

I elected to end the war. Closer to sunset the birds were in for the night. The nursery was quiet. My plan...new times for watering and plant grooming. For quick access the trash bins were repositioned out of the back yard to the far side of my truck closer to the street. And finally, make use of my front door instead of the back. **In essence**, I pretty much adjusted everything for needs of the birds.

Even so every time going out my front door, all the fences, trees, and various other locations were surveyed for any signs of birds. To get to my truck, I walked quickly out on the street in front of my house, opened the door, and promptly got in. Somehow, the mockingbird clan seemed to understand my truck was important to me or at the very least, I was leaving them alone.

But come on!!! I do have to come out my back door sometimes. After all it was my house, I kept telling myself. So, I went out my back door.

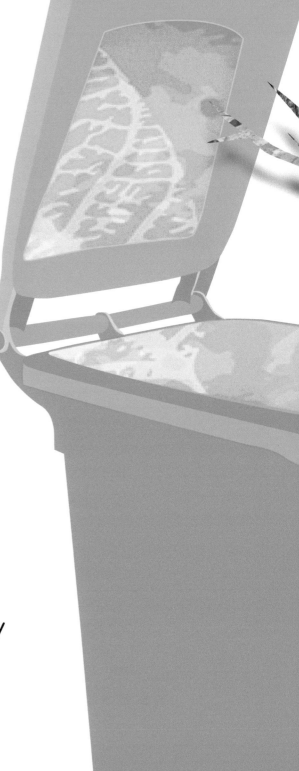

To my surprise the nest was briefly quiet without mom or dad, just babies.

Where were they. . .?

Was Mr. actually baiting me?

Was it a trap?

He can't be that smart, can he?

Still standing on the back porch, oddly neither of them showed up. Tip toeing down the stairs, I sneaked quietly to the nest. Inside were three somewhat pink babies just beginning to grow their feathers. As soon they saw me, they all stopped moving around and peeping. Certainly not any room to move in that bed.

Nature is soooo amazing.

How exciting!

I actually got to see them.

Silently creeping away there was a great sense of satisfaction. Several weeks went by with babies chirping for their daily food.

Did I win...for once?

Mom or dad flew out coming back with a worm or bug. They were working hard to feed those babies. For now, there was no bird interaction as long as my avoidance plan remained intact.

Life was harmonious and happy again. . .at least for them.

At some point, not sure exactly when, mom and dad were not at the nest or flying around any more. Everything was very quiet. Wonder what was going on?

Do I dare check out the nest, I asked myself.

Ok, I'm going to do it!!!

To my surprise the nest was completely empty. Babies were gone...onto their new birdie life. Hallelujah!!! Still looking around the whole time, **I tore the nest down as fast as I could.**
Threw that thing right in the trash.
What a feeling of accomplishment. It was over.

Now my life can go back to normal!

Interestingly enough, Mr. mockingbird
flew in several times after his kids
took off to see what I was up to.
Just outside my bougainvillea, a few
feet away he perched on his favorite
tree limb. With full view of me, he
could see whatever I was doing.

Once with a worm
hanging out of his mouth,
head turned slightly,
he just sat watching me.

The look in his eyes
was different,
as if he was
actually happy, and
maybe...even a nice bird.
But because previously
he had been so obnoxious,
I told him waving my arm outward,

"Go away!   Go away!"

A different full-blown summer day about 102
degrees there he was sitting on the same branch.
His mouth was wide open panting away in the heat
of the day. Funny, I didn't know birds panted.
"Silly bird go somewhere its cooler," I told him.
He sat for a few more minutes and flew off.

Was he was trying to be my friend?
His eyes were friendly and inquisitive.
Did he actually like me? I wonder?

Some time went by and here came the same male mockingbird
again sitting on the fence ...only this time glaring at me. Even
though all mockingbirds pretty much look alike, I knew this bird
by his demeanor, habits, and stares. Giving him no attention, I
got in my truck leaving for work. The following day was watering
time for my plants in the front yard. Mind you, **not** by the
bougainvillea. Unexpecting as I was... almost immediately
something was on my back. I ducked down walking swiftly
toward the front door. Looking over my shoulder, sure
enough **he was back.** My mind started racing.

They don't even have a nest?
Or do they???

My community is a friendly one.

My neighbor and a fellow bird lover spotted a **newly built nest.**

Did you see it he asked me?

No Way! **After looking,** Oh, yes, they did.

Nest number 3 was situated very low and openly exposed in the bougainvillea. It was close to the street for easy access. Of course, Mr. put it right next to my truck and now close to the front yard. Like the last time there were three eggs in the nest--- soon to become loud and lively babies filling it. There was no way for me to live with these birds now.

Inside my house during the day, the many peeps of hungry baby birds were heard. Out my kitchen window facing my carport, I saw mom and dad taking turns flying in and out feeding them. They were good parents attending to the need of their little ones.

But this nest was directly in my living space.

By bird standards if I got too close, I suffered for it. As you can imagine this happened frequently. If I went to my truck, trash, yard, or for that matter anywhere . . . with no hesitation hubby was coming at me.

Wifey getting a visual of me **sounded the alarm**. Then both were sounding the alarm. The call would start with one bird and then echo back and forth between the two. Sometimes, in the nearby area other mockingbird alarms were going off. Some to the left and some to the right.

They seemed to be saying. . .

Dive

Dive

Dive

At that point, who would be coming you know birds recruit help this couple did. Big family knew? Everyone was on the haven't seen the movie "Birds."

I wasn't sure at me. Did . . .well they do!!! At least with lots of relatives. Who lookout for **ME**. And no, I Things changed even more.

Because we had history, now **I was his number one target**. It didn't make any difference where I went--out the door, to the street, or in the yard. This male mockingbird was doing his best to get rid of me. Any time outside. . . anywhere. . . I had to constantly scour the area for a visual of my assailant. Once spotted coming in for an attack, I faced him waiving my arms, broom, jacket, shovel, or whatever I had in my hand at the time. Whenever possible, I would take some evasive maneuvers--ducking and covering my head and face as best as possible. All the while yelling "Go away!!!" Oh, of course and glaring back trying to make eye contact with this insane bird. **Intimidation, you know.**

You would think shear human size alone would be daunting to a small sized bird. Nope, nothing scared him off. He just came back around again and again like a plane circling to land. Early on I learned to never turn my back on this bird. And if I didn't see him which was often...I always paid for it. Mr. was so relentless that even when bending down to prune or water, you guessed it...he hit me in the butt. As long as he got me somewhere his objective was successful.

I started calling him "Diver."

This little maniac was unstoppable. Really think he has lost his mind. The next few weeks went by with incessant diving. Diver didn't care what my location was now. He just flew around looking for me to dive. I was the enemy. This ridiculous bird dove at me, and then dove at me again just because he could. Over and over hitting me wherever he wanted.

35

Had this become a game for him? For me it was frightening, exhausting, and very maddening. In all my many attempts to get away from this bird, I'm sure my neighbors thought I was losing my mind. Out in the yard with broom, stick, or anything else handy batting at the air trying furiously to get him away from me. Or if the hose happened to be in my hands, spraying the air. My intent was to scare him. Of course, I never did.

Diver was way too fast.

And then I had to raise my voice. I was mad. Diver was so infuriating, any normal person would be hollering. Sometimes I actually think he was laughing at me as he flew away.

What a fool I must have looked like!!!

36

Life was so unbearable I dreaded going to my truck or trying to put my trash on the street. Reaching out to my son-in-law whose dad knows everything there is to know about birds, one solution came. His advice was for me to play the calls of other mockingbirds every time I went out my back door. He sent me a soundtrack. Good... maybe Diver will think there are other birds and be scared away.

I was all charged up and ready for battle.

Stepping out on the back porch with my iPad in hand, I played the bird calls from the sound track. Diver sitting on the fence as usual, had his back to me. He turned around quickly facing me, tipped his head to one side, and listened intently.

At last I'm getting some results. I'm so pleased!!!

But then he sat up straight, got all excited, and **fluffed out all his feathers.** He started singing with it.

Guess what. . .Diver liked it.

I was so mad. Back in the house defeated. I hate this bird. I really do.

I was losing this battle.

Repeatedly diving at my ears, head, back, shoulders, and various other places of my body was unnerving. My fear was that at any moment he would make serious contact.

Talons

You know birds have talons and beaks
that can both do damage. It scared me.
His beady little black eyes would try to pierce through me.
Such a small bird and so intimidating.

It didn't help when my daughter told me the story about a man who come to
E.R. with an owl attached to his head. The talons of the bird were stuck in
his head. They couldn't get them out... so the man and the bird came to the
emergency room. Afterwards I couldn't get the thoughts of mockingbird
talons stuck in my head. Not a comfortable image to be mulling around.

If that wasn't enough, Diver kept getting closer and closer to my back door by scooting along the fence toward me. He would glare as if daring me and then hop one hop closer. **Hop and Glare. Is this a game he played?** I didn't like it. This bird can't be smarter than me.
I was bewildered and unsure
about the whole thing but...
what could I do?

Beaks

It got so bad, once with my back door open, I actually thought he was going to follow me inside the house to dive me.
The nerve of this bird.

Really!!!

I found myself staying inside my house more than usual. Needless to say, with the back door closed tight.

The dog door was cut into the same back door. Jazz was in and out frequently. Strangely enough this particular bird could care less about my 50lb boxer. I always thought birds were afraid of dogs. No, not so with Diver.

He was after me and me alone!

This little 8" bird was creating so much misery. How much of this can I take? The diving seemed like it would never stop.

In my agony, I shared all my troubles with the girls at work again. Telling them how mad this bird made me and how he would dive me over and over.

They just laughed.

41

I didn't think it was funny.
Not at all. I had had it!

My nephew, the bird hunter, would he come over
and shoot this wild mockingbird?
When asked he laughed at me and said,
    "No I won't.
They are way too quick."

Not to mention that I had completely forgotten...
in a mobilehome park there are windows on all four
sides and in all four directions.
There would be no clear shot anyway.

Can't seem to win.

No matter what...
    it always backfired.

One good thing, whenever I did make it to my truck, the babies in the nest were visible. Three fat fully feathered chicks filled the entire small nest. I wondered, it was so small. Maybe so they wouldn't fall out . . . no room to move anywhere. As it turned out, this couple didn't choose a safe spot for their 3rd family. Early one morning my neighbor told me some animal got into the nest.

The babies were gone.

Probably a cat.

How sad

This time I tore the nest down but with sadness. **I had grown accustomed to their company.**

Life can change so quickly.

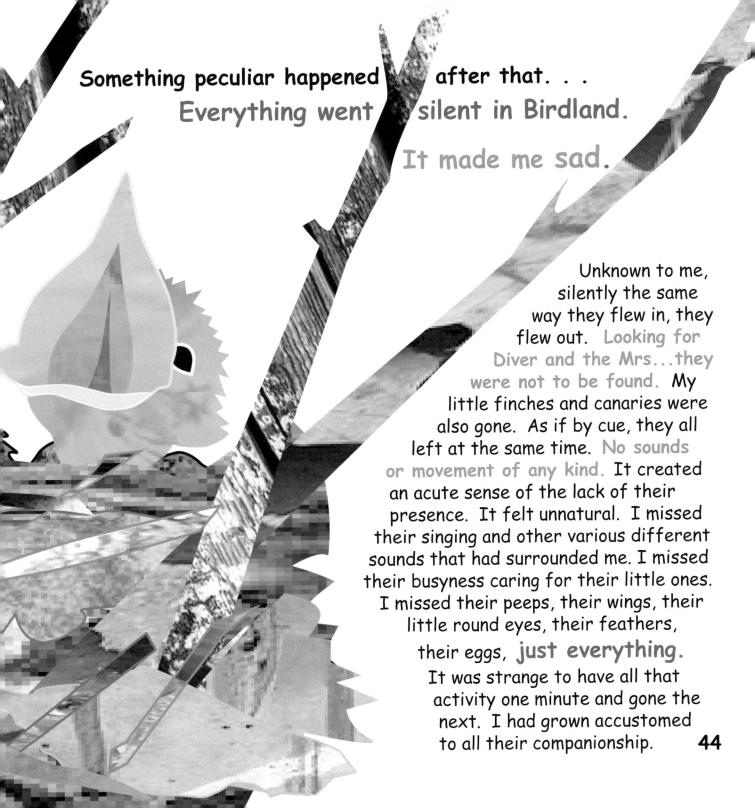

Something peculiar happened after that. . .
Everything went silent in Birdland.

It made me sad.

Unknown to me, silently the same way they flew in, they flew out. Looking for Diver and the Mrs...they were not to be found. My little finches and canaries were also gone. As if by cue, they all left at the same time. No sounds or movement of any kind. It created an acute sense of the lack of their presence. It felt unnatural. I missed their singing and other various different sounds that had surrounded me. I missed their busyness caring for their little ones. I missed their peeps, their wings, their little round eyes, their feathers, their eggs, just everything.

It was strange to have all that activity one minute and gone the next. I had grown accustomed to all their companionship. **44**

Mad
mode

For this reason, sadly I had a reprieve. Actually go to my truck, my yard, and my trash bins without a mockingbird diving me. Didn't have to protect my head or be on the lookout every time I stepped out my house.

Everything remained very quiet outside for a short time.

Searching daily, there were still no signs of the couple. I wondered if they broke up...you know like people when something bad happens. Were Mr. and Mrs. off somewhere crying? If I had lost my babies I would be mourning. How weird, I felt sorrow for the lost babies and for the parents who lost them. I love birds and yes even these mockingbirds.

Trying so hard to learn to live with them.

Now what?

A few weeks of silence went by. Guess what? Diver and the Mrs. were sitting together again on the back fence just as if nothing had happened. They were scouting for a new nest location. Everyone seemed to be fine, happy, and on a task. I don't know if they figured out their babies were safer in a tree, but thank goodness, they choose my crepe myrtle tree.

The two were busy building their 4th nest. They were fairly fast. Once completed, Diver went to his post. He sat on the fence glaring at me.

Just like before he was on duty, angry, and in ATTACK mode.

Man was I in for it

After further research... mockingbirds lay 4-5 sets of babies in one season. This was number 4. Ok, enough is enough! Things had to change.

Their natural predator is the hoot owl. Ah hah, maybe that's it. I ordered two life size shiny hoot owls with big yellow eyes. Noisy bells hung from the bottom. At the hardware store I bought connectors to let the owls twirl freely in the wind. Tied to the bottom branch of their nesting tree,

bells were ringing, hoot owl twirling, and eyes were peering.

47

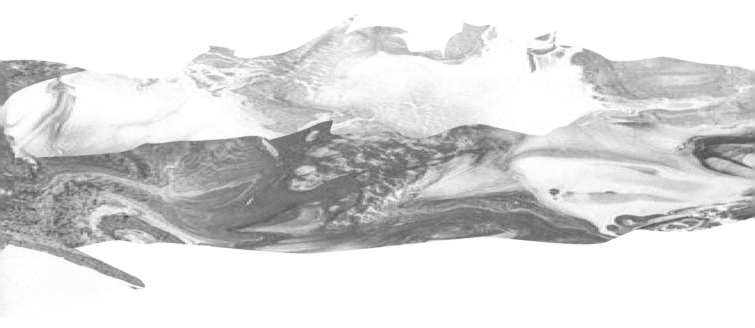

He looked at the owl
Diver did not like it at all

He sat on the fence trying to decide if he
would dive me. He wanted to,
really really wanted to. But he paused.
He looked at the owl, then at me
and then at the owl again.

With a very different look in his eyes this time.
Fear, I think. He flew in to dive me several times
but when he saw the owl. . .flew right back out.

This is awesome...I think I finally won!   **48**

At last life could be normal again.

I could use my own yard, take my trash out… you know walk to my truck… normal stuff. Their babies grew untouched and flew away as nature planned. Going about my chores there was no interference from mockingbirds. No ducking or on the lookout all the time. This time Diver respected the distance and the space between us.

He kept his eyes on that owl.

Success…it was wonderful.

I felt freedom from oppression.

Even though the babies were gone, mom and dad were still flying around frequently. Diver flew in alone occasionally, just to see what I was doing. Sometimes he would just watch me. Each time, he made sure I saw him too before flying off. I finally figured out he wanted me to acknowledge him somehow. I tried looking back at him making eye contact. He was ok with that. Sitting in different trees around my house he started peeping at me.

One day he flew into my front yard landing on the ground in front of me so I couldn't miss him. As soon as I looked at him, **he was happy, spread his wings and flew off.** It seemed almost like he was trying to play with me. His eyes were kind and curious.

I think he might like me now. Go figure!

A month has gone by since the female flew off. I took the noisy twirling owl down and put it in my shed. May have to use it again, hope not. **Diver never left**. He continues to fly around the neighborhood doing what birds do. Occasionally he comes down on his favorite tree branch **to check me out.** Yesterday he landed in the bougainvillea, his old roost. From different places around my mobilehome, I could hear a mockingbird chirping at me. I finally paid attention to which bird was calling out. Diver was peeping at me. It seemed like he was telling me, **"I'm still here."** All the while, respecting me like a normal bird keeping a healthy distance. Because of my deep affection for birds, I started to enjoy his companionship.

Diver doesn't dive me when he is happy or off duty

So nice and refreshing

One day while watering the roses, he flew by and peeped at me. Positioned low in the sky, only a short distance in front of me, he made sure I saw him. Landing on a nearby fence, he continued to peep, a happy peep. Realizing he wanted me to interact with him, I said **"Diver is that you? How are you?"** He turned toward me, tipped his head slightly to one side, and stopped peeping. His eyes were friendly, and he seemed excited I was talking to him.

I guess we are friends now. Not sure how that happened!!! ...but he likes me. **Even weirder I like him too!**

52

Both Diver and I know he has claimed my yard as his. He doesn't have any plans to live anywhere else. As I reflected back over the last few months and my relationship with this bird...an understanding came to me. Diver never hurt me. For that matter didn't even try to. He certainly had plenty of times he could have laid into me. I think always his intent was to get me to leave. He was on duty and his number one job was to protect his babies. Funny, I was never aware of that when he was diving me. I wonder what other things I didn't realize about him.

The internet tells me mockingbirds live for 8 years. I have no idea what to expect next year. After much consideration, I have decided to watch diligently for nest building season in the next upcoming spring.

Diver has given me quite the education.

Nature is definitely full of lots of surprises. I have to say I love it and look forward to the future as we dwell together.

Until next year!!!

The End, NOT!!!

Now ask the animals, and let them teach you that God does not deal with His creatures according to their character; And ask the birds of the air, and let them tell you; Or speak to the earth with its many forms of life, and it will teach you; And let the fish of the sea declare this truth to you. Who among all these does not recognize in all these things that good and evil are randomly scattered throughout nature and human life; That the hand of the Lord has done this, in whose hand is the life of every living thing, and the breath of all mankind. Job 12:7-10

My Story

My mobilehome park has trees scattered throughout. It is amazing how many different types of bird end up here. The crepe myrtle tree and bougainvillea literally give me a wall of greenery. Needless to say, it attracts many birds. I never planned it that way, but nature took full advantage. In the beginning, I really tried diligently to co-inhabit with this fearless dad. I was doing my best, but it wasn't working. It soon became an impossible feat. I was fearful of going out my back door. As the days ticked by, my dislike for the bird grew. He was intimidating and relentless in all his many attacks. Reaching out to my family and friends on numerous occasions, I tried everything recommended, but to no avail. Throughout this chaotic journey, they kept telling me over and over and over **"Write a story about this bird, it's funny."** To which I told them, **"No way, I can't stand this bird. He is making my life miserable. Why would I write a story about him? And I don't think it is funny!"** I really meant it. They just laughed as I shared the latest battle. Attack after attack, I was done with this mockingbird. Then, I just wanted him out of my life. But it has been an amazing journey experiencing his moods and watching the different hats he wears. I can see it clearly now. After the babies were gone and his mate flew away, Diver becomes a completely different bird. Taking on the responsibility of being a dad he became a warrior going to battle.

With his family taken care of he wore the hat of curiosity and playfulness, absolutely the opposite. Mockingbirds in general are known for mimicking sounds like car alarms and singing them . . . **over and over all night**. Diver is not a bird that sings **keeping me awake** --- like the poor next door neighbor. For that I am thankful. I came to the realization all birds are not carbon copies. **Anyone that tells you all birds are the same has never met Diver.** In the very essence of a bird is something regal and majestic. **My love for birds** remains and even continues to grow. I can't quite put my finger on it, but I know that **God's birds are unique** and life giving. **They are incredibly special.**

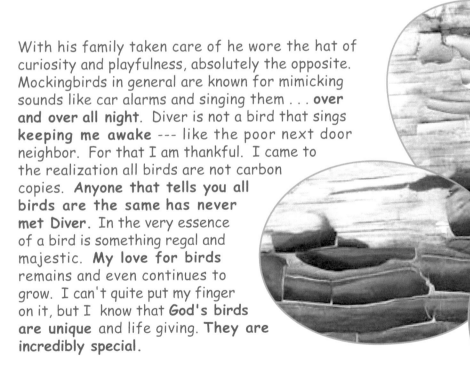

Diver

58

Copyright © 2023 Londa Ogden.

All rights reserved. No part of this book may be used or reproduced by any means, graphic, electronic, or mechanical, including photocopying, recording, taping or by any information storage retrieval system without the written permission of the author except in the case of brief quotations embodied in critical articles and reviews.

WestBow Press books may be ordered through booksellers or by contacting:

WestBow Press
A Division of Thomas Nelson & Zondervan
1663 Liberty Drive
Bloomington, IN 47403
www.westbowpress.com
844-714-3454

Because of the dynamic nature of the Internet, any web addresses or links contained in this book may have changed since publication and may no longer be valid. The views expressed in this work are solely those of the author and do not necessarily reflect the views of the publisher, and the publisher hereby disclaims any responsibility for them.

Scripture taken from the King James Version of the Bible.

ISBN: 978-1-6642-9057-0 (sc)
ISBN: 978-1-6642-9058-7 (hc)
ISBN: 978-1-6642-9056-3 (e)

Library of Congress Control Number: 2023901612

Print information available on the last page.

WestBow Press rev. date: 08/23/2023

WestBow
PRESS®
A DIVISION OF THOMAS NELSON
& ZONDERVAN

Printed in the United States
by Baker & Taylor Publisher Services